D0466403

BRODART

1/08

The Massachusetts Bay Colony: The Puritans Arrive From England

Mitchell Lane
PUBLISHERS

P.O. Box 196 • Hockessin, Delaware 19707

Titles in the Series

Georgia: The Debtors Colony

Holidays and Celebrations
in Colonial America

Jamestown: The First English Colony

The Massachusetts Bay Colony:
The Puritans Arrive from England

New Netherland: The Dutch
Settle the Hudson Valley

Pennsylvania: William Penn and
the City of Brotherly Love

The Plymouth Colony: The Pilgrims
Settle in New England

The Massachusetts Bay Colony: The Puritans Arrive From England

Bonnie Hinman

Printing   1   2   3   4   5   6   7   8   9

Library of Congress Cataloging-in-Publication Data
Hinman, Bonnie.
  The Massachusetts Bay Colony: The Puritans arrive from England / by Bonnie Hinman.
      p. cm.—(Building America)
  Includes bibliographical references and index.
  ISBN 1-58415-460-8 (library bound)
    1. Massachusetts—History—Colonial period, ca. 1600–1775—Juvenile literature.
2. Massachusetts Bay Company—Juvenile literature. 3. Puritans—Massachusetts—
History—17th century—Juvenile literature. I. Title. II. Building America (Hockessin, Del.)
F67.H55 2007
974.4'02—dc22
                                                                              2006006097
ISBN-10:1-58415-460-8   ISBN-13: 978-1-58415-460-0

ABOUT THE AUTHOR: Bonnie Hinman, a writer for over thirty years, finds the Puritans of Massachusetts to be remarkable people. She also enjoys learning about the Native Americans who helped the settlers. Bonnie graduated from Missouri State University and has taught creative writing at Crowder College. Her books for Mitchell Lane Publishers include *Florence Nightingale and the Advancement of Nursing, The Life and Times of William Penn,* and *Pennsylvania: William Penn and the City of Brotherly Love.* Her book *A Stranger in His Own House: The Story of W.E.B. Du Bois* (Morgan Reynolds) was chosen for the 2006 New York Public Library's Books for the Teen Age. She lives in Joplin, Missouri, with her husband, Bill, two cats, and three dogs.

PHOTO CREDITS: Cover, pp. 1, 3—North Wind; pp. 15, 24, 39—Library of Congress; p. 6—Massachusetts Historical Society; pp. 12, 20, 34—Sharon Beck; p. 18—Bettman/ CORBIS; p. 26—British Library; p. 29—Rijks Museum; p. 31—New York Historical Society; p. 41—Constitution Society.

PUBLISHER'S NOTE: This story is based on the author's extensive research, which she believes to be accurate. Documentation of such research is contained on page 46.
    The internet sites referenced herein were active as of the publication date. Due to the fleeting nature of some web sites, we cannot guarantee they will all be active when you are reading this book.

Contents

*For Your Information

John Winthrop, Puritan founder of Massachusetts Bay Colony, appears to be dressed in a fancy way, with his white ruff and gloves. Actually he is dressed plainly compared to the elaborate fashions of his time.

Chapter

1

"The Citty Upon a Hill"

John Winthrop and an exploring party set off from Salem shortly after arriving in the New World in June 1630. They traveled south along the coast of Massachusetts Bay. They were looking for just the right spot to settle the shiploads of people who had traveled from England to make a new life in America.

The boat sloshed through the bay and into a quieter harbor as it twisted between islands and turned west. Several sailors manned the small boat while Winthrop and the other men kept their eyes on the coastline. Most of what they saw on shore must have pleased them very much. There were beaches broken by coves, and fingers of land jutting out into the water. Beyond the shore were rolling hills.

The explorers pushed through the harbor past the peninsula that the Indians called Shawmut and into one of two rivers that fed the harbor. The Mystic River flowed into the harbor from the northwest, and the Charles came in from the southwest. Winthrop's party sailed up the Mystic for five or six miles and found what they were looking for.

Broad acres of land had already been burned off—then abandoned—by Indians, and there were plenty of freshwater streams. It was a perfect place for their new community. The men didn't linger but headed back to Salem to tell the others the good news.

The area around what would become Boston Harbor wasn't totally uninhabited. There were a few hardy settlers on the peninsulas and islands. Most of them were left over from previous settlement attempts. They offered what help they could to their prospective new neighbors—although they may not have been entirely happy with the idea of having hundreds of people descending on their pristine lands.

Back in Salem, the news of a perfect place to settle was greeted with mixed reactions. Thomas Dudley, who was the deputy governor, led several of the other leaders to insist on further exploration. Dudley and Winthrop were to have a rocky future together as they established the Bay Colony, and it may have started with this first disagreement.

The colonists had intended to settle at Cape Ann, farther north on the coast near Salem. It's not known for sure why Winthrop and Dudley decided to look for a new spot. The Cape Ann peninsula had been sparsely settled as a fishing and farming community. Its residents could offer advice to the newcomers.

That advice in early summer 1630 might have been to go right back to England. Salem's residents had just passed through a terrible winter. Many of them were malnourished and sick. Dudley later wrote, "We found the Colony in a sad and unexpected condition." He added: "many of those alive weak and sick" and "all the corn and bread amongst them all hardly sufficient to feed them a fortnight."[1]

It's possible that the grim aspect these settlers presented may have convinced Winthrop and Dudley that it would be better to find a place where there were fewer reminders of the harshness of the Massachusetts winter. It is just as likely that they didn't find enough room at Salem, for there were between three hundred and four hundred families who would need land and homes. Dudley wrote simply, "Salem, where we landed, pleased us not."[2]

Governor Winthrop had given a sermon on board the ship *Arabella* that would often be quoted. He laid out before his fellow passengers his ideas about what they would build in the New World. The most famous sentence is actually borrowed from the Bible. Using the spelling that was common then, Winthrop said, "Wee shall be as a Citty upon a Hill."[3]

He meant that the Puritan settlers would found both a physical city and a religious community whose standards others could look up to. Religion was much more than just a Sunday practice for Puritans. Their entire lives revolved around their churches and their faith in the Bible.

The fleet of ships loaded up again at Salem and sailed south to the harbor. The leaders had compromised and chosen a site on Charleston Peninsula, across the Charles River from Shawmut. It was quickly apparent that Winthrop's "Citty upon a Hill" was not going to flourish. There wasn't enough good water around Charleston and probably not enough land. By late July, small groups began leaving Charleston to found towns along the Charles and Mystic Rivers and elsewhere around the harbor.

Disease caught up with the settlers, and that was one reason they decided to disperse. Another was the difficulty they would have defending their position if attacked by the French, who were also try- ing to establish settlements. The Puritans were too weak to fortify their position at Charleston. If they spread out, disease might decrease; and if the French did attack, at least some of them would live.

This was exactly the opposite approach to settlement that Winthrop had cherished, but to his credit, he was flexible enough to change his plans. He may have considered this just a temporary measure. Winter was coming, and the settlers needed shelters and the opportunity to find sources of food. Winthrop and other leaders did what they could to maintain control of the new colony by holding court, assessing taxes, and appointing constables.

By the beginning of September, small groups of settlers had moved across the harbor to Shawmut. The peninsula hadn't been the destination for any of the larger, more organized groups that had gone up the rivers to settle. It was fairly small and more open to attack from the sea. Gradually, however, more settlers began to settle there.

Shawmut was given the official English name of Boston. Winthrop and Dudley moved to the settlement, bringing the government with them. By the end of October, the population in Boston had grown to around 150. The church that had been started in Charleston moved by the end of December. It became the First Church of Boston.

The first winter for the new Massachusetts Bay colonists wasn't easy. They fought disease and malnutrition because they had arrived too late in the year to plant crops. They survived on leftover salted meat from their journey, along with shellfish and whatever other food they could scrounge. Scurvy was common, and some people froze to death. In many cases the settlers lived in tents or bark wigwams, which offered little protection from the bitter cold that arrived just after Christmas. As many as 200 of the nearly 1,000 settlers who came with Winthrop's fleet died before spring.

Governor Winthrop gave freely of his own provisions and paid for food that could be found for sale in other settlements. He also dispatched the ship back to England for supplies. By February, the colonists faced dire conditions as the food was practically gone. Finally, a ship arrived from England, bringing supplies and, with them, hope.

Lemon juice cured the scurvy but couldn't cure the discouraged spirits of some settlers. Other ships arrived with provisions, but they didn't return to England empty. During the first year at least 100 colonists sailed back to their homeland.

They may have given up too early, for the food shortage was over by spring, and the colonists got busy planting crops and building permanent homes. The Massachusetts Bay Colony government tightened control over the scattered towns but allowed more people to vote. Winthrop was reelected governor in May 1631. Puritan churches were established in every town. Once a man became a member of the church, he could vote on government issues.

After the first hard winter, Massachusetts Bay Colony prospered. It appeared that Winthrop's idea of building "a Citty upon a Hill" was not such an impossible dream after all.

Scurvy

Scurvy was well known as a disease long before John Winthrop wrote in his journal of that first hard winter in the Bay Colony. "The poorer sort of people (who lay long in tents, etc.) were much afflicted with the scurvy, and many died, especially at Boston and Charlestown: but when this ship came and brought stores of juice of lemons, many recovered speedily."[4] The ship he mentioned was the *Lyon*, which arrived with supplies in February 1631.

Scurvy is caused by a lack of vitamin C, but this wasn't known until 1932. It particularly afflicted sailors and others who were away from normal food supplies for a long time. Symptoms are weakness and joint pain. It can also cause bleeding gums and bruises on the skin. If left untreated, it is fatal.

Although scurvy's cause wasn't understood, remedies existed, as Winthrop mentioned in his journal. Sailors began to carry lime and lemon juice on long journeys; sauerkraut was also found to prevent the disease. James Lind, a Scottish physician who served as a ship's surgeon in the 1740s, undertook an experiment to discover the most effective treatment for scurvy. Eighty out of 350 sailors on board the HMS *Salisbury* were sick with scurvy when the ship landed in Plymouth, Massachusetts, in 1746. He selected twelve of the suffering men and divided them into six pairs. Each pair was given a different remedy along with their regular food. The remedies included cider, vinegar, seawater, an unknown elixir, and a combination of garlic, mustard, and horseradish. The sixth pair ate two oranges and one lemon every day.

Ship's surgeon James Lind tends scurvy patients during his experiment to determine the best treatment for the disease.

The sailors given cider reported a slight improvement, but the two who had eaten the citrus fruits had a miraculous recovery. Lind proved that citrus fruits were superior to any other remedy. His experiment laid the groundwork for the discovery of vitamins.

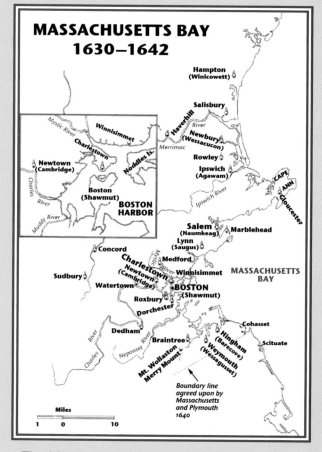

MASSACHUSETTS BAY 1630–1642

Hampton (Winicowett)

Salisbury

Mystic River

Winnisimmet

Haverhill River

Newbury (Wessacucon)

Merrimac

Charlestown

Noddles Is.

Newtown (Cambridge)

Rowley

Ipswich (Agawam)

CAPE ANN

Gloucester

Charles River

Boston (Shawmut)

BOSTON HARBOR

Ipswich River

Muddy River

Salem (Naumkeag)

Marblehead

Lynn (Saugus)

Concord

Medford

Mystic River

Charlestown

Newtown (Cambridge)

Winnisimmet

MASSACHUSETTS BAY

Sudbury

Watertown

BOSTON (Shawmut)

Roxbury

Dorchester

River

Dedham

Charles River

Neponset River

Braintree

Cohasset

Hingham (Barecove)

Weymouth (Wessagusset)

Scituate

Mt. Wollaston Merry Mount

Boundary line agreed upon by Massachusetts and Plymouth 1640

Miles

1   0   10

The Massachusetts Bay area in the 1600s. A few of these towns existed before the Puritans arrived in 1630, but most were founded by the Puritans in the following 10 years.

Chapter

②

Leaving the Old World for the New

Englishmen had been coming to America to settle for at least twenty years before the Massachusetts Bay Colony was founded. The most famous of these settlements was Plymouth Colony, settled in 1620 by the separatist Puritan group called the Pilgrims. The *Mayflower* carried 102 passengers to their new home on Plymouth Bay in November 1620. After a horrible winter of sickness and starvation, only half were alive to see spring arrive.

The Plymouth Colony soon received their first Indian visitors, who provided the crucial assistance that allowed the colony to endure. Samoset came first and later brought Massasoit, chief of the Wampanoag people, whose territory lay south of Plymouth along Narragansett Bay. Massasoit was received with great respect. He repaid the honor by leaving behind another Indian, Squanto, to help the Pilgrims. Squanto showed the settlers how and when to plant crops, as well as where to fish. His help may have been the key to their survival.

Land was usually obtained by way of land grants given by the rulers of England. In 1620, King James I gave all of what we know as New England to a group of noblemen. This group in turn granted a charter to the New England Company, which eventually became the Massachusetts Bay Company. These companies were formed by investors who wanted to send representatives to the New World to settle there. The plan was for these settlers to send products for sale quickly back to England, making a tidy profit for the investors.

Colonists had been sent to the Massachusetts Bay area before John Winthrop and his group arrived in 1630. However, most of them eventually returned to England—if they had survived. The first group from the Massachusetts Bay Company arrived in 1629 and built a town at Salem. This was the hungry and sick group that met Winthrop and Dudley when their ships arrived at Cape Ann. The right combination of place and people and money for supplies just hadn't happened yet.

The Massachusetts Bay Company was formed by Puritan merchants. Puritans were a religious group who found the established Church of England, also called the Anglican Church, to be overly concerned with ritual and hierarchy. The Puritans wanted to do away with any ritual, ceremony, or organizational structure that was not specifically mentioned in the Bible. The moral code that guided their lives was based on the Bible and their interpretation of the laws of God and the teachings of Jesus. There were different groups of Puritans in the sixteenth century; the ones who formed the Bay Company were willing to remain in the Anglican Church if it could be "purified."

The Puritans were often persecuted for their beliefs. Times might be better or worse for them depending on who was the king or queen of England at the time. Queen Elizabeth I, who reigned from 1558 to 1603, strengthened England's military, which helped bring peace and prosperity to her country. She encouraged a broad English church and found no need to eliminate or persecute religious minorities. She also cooperated with Parliament, unlike many of the kings and queens who came before her. James I was Elizabeth's successor and continued her moderate approach.

The climate changed drastically when Charles I became king in 1625 upon the death of his father. Charles had no sympathy for Puritans. He did two things in particular that caused the Puritans much grief. He dissolved Parliament and refused to recall it for many years, and he appointed William Laud to be Bishop of London.

Queen Elizabeth I (1533–1603) was popular with most of her subjects. Well educated and smart, she could speak five languages. Some of her favorite pastimes were horse riding, hunting, hawking, and watching sporting events such as jousting. She also loved music, dancing, and the theater. The Puritans did not approve. They thought these pursuits impious.

Parliament often had Puritan members, so it was considered a moderating influence on the king. With Parliament permanently out of session, King Charles was free to run England without interference. Bishop Laud was a strict Anglican. He tightened the rules governing all worship and ministers to the point that Puritans could hardly worship according to their beliefs.

This tense political and religious atmosphere in England in the 1620s was the last straw for many Puritans. They had been devoted to saving the church from within by working for reform. Now it looked to many of them that they'd be better off moving to the New World and starting a new Puritan society there.

John Winthrop was one of these Puritans. He hated to give up on his native country but finally decided that he could do more good for God in America. Preparations for the move took some time, as Winthrop had property to sell and a family to care for. In the end he had to leave his wife and younger children behind in the care of his eldest son. The son would tend to the sale of the property and then take the family to join Winthrop in Massachusetts.

During the months of consultation with other prospective colonists and with the directors of the Massachusetts Bay Company, Winthrop showed that he was an organized and shrewd manager. With these qualities in mind, the company made him governor of the new colony.

Because of an oversight in the royal charter granted to the Massachusetts Bay Company, the government of Massachusetts was free to be administered by those living in the new land. Usually the king required that the directors of a company meet in London, where he could exert control. When this requirement was left out of the charter, the company directors promptly voted to make the meeting place in Massachusetts.

The Massachusetts Bay Colony had no more bad winters after the first. The colonists planted crops, built permanent homes, and established trade with other colonies and with the local Indians.

The Indian population had been greatly reduced in this area by terrible epidemics, probably smallpox and measles, just a few years before Englishmen started pouring into the New England coast. What was tragic for the Indians benefited the colonists. Not only was there less potential trouble from Indians who would have wanted to protect their land, but the land that the Indians had used for raising crops was now available for the settlers. Winthrop's group found acres of land already cleared of brush for planting but not being used by anyone. This let the planting begin much sooner than might otherwise have happened.

Newcomers to the Massachusetts Bay Colony were slow to arrive in the first couple of years, but by 1635, the trickle of immigrants had become a flood. Over 2,000 people, chiefly Puritans, arrived each year, usually in Boston Harbor. This tide of new settlers was mostly in response to problems at home for the Puritans. Bishop Laud had been promoted to Archbishop of Canterbury, which gave him even more power. He used this power to try to bring the Puritans back into line with the Church of England.

Puritans reacted by packing up in huge numbers and moving across the ocean in what became known as the Great Migration. They brought with them new money and skills that the colony could use for growth. It was a time of prosperity for almost all colonists.

Economically things were going well, but Winthrop and the other leaders found it harder to keep religious matters under control. Two people challenged the orthodox beliefs that Governor Winthrop and the governing body, called the General Court, tried hard to maintain.

Roger Williams had come to America with Winthrop's fleet and had been a respected Puritan. However, his religious beliefs had changed, causing him to clash with Winthrop and the General Court. When he preached or held meetings at his home, he called for the absolute separation of church and state. This was in direct opposition to the Bay Colony's fundamental position. Williams was loud and rather tactless in expressing his views, and the General Court didn't waste much time before banishing him from the colony in January 1636.

The uproar over Williams had barely died down when another nonconformist came to the attention of Puritan authorities. Anne Hutchinson had immigrated to America in 1634 with her husband, William, and eleven of their children. Hutchinson had always been an intelligent, persuasive woman who thought for herself in all matters, including religion. This independence had led her to question some basic Puritan beliefs.

The Church of England and the Puritans believed in a doctrine they called the Covenant of Works. Under this covenant, people believed that the only way to get to heaven was to follow church rules closely to keep from sinning, and to do many good deeds.

Hutchinson and some Puritan ministers believed that a person couldn't do enough good works to earn God's love and forgiveness. They thought that people were saved by having complete faith in God, and not by doing good works. Soon Hutchinson was hosting meetings in her home in Boston to talk about sermons and to discuss the Covenant of Grace, as the belief was called.

It was trickier for Bay Colony leaders to silence Hutchinson than it had been to get rid of Roger Williams. They thought of her as just a woman who would soon settle down. They underestimated her intelligence and quick wits. Hutchinson could win almost any argument with her debating abilities.

17

The Massachusetts Colony General Court members were surprised to find that Anne Hutchinson could effectively defend herself at her trial. However, her skill did not save her from being convicted of heresy.

Hutchinson had powerful supporters. The Massachusetts Bay Colony elected its governor each year, and the governorship passed around often in the early years. In spring 1636, Sir Henry Vane was elected governor over Winthrop. Vane admired and respected Hutchinson. He didn't take any action when she began holding prayer meetings in her home, during which she criticized the ministers and their orthodox beliefs in the Covenant of Works.

The matter didn't come to a head until 1637 when Winthrop was reelected governor. In November, Hutchinson was put on trial before the General Court. She defended herself vigorously but was found to be a heretic and was sentenced to banishment from the colony. Since she was pregnant and the harsh winter was just beginning, the banishment was postponed until spring.

Spring 1638 found Hutchinson and her family and some other supporters on the road to Providence, Rhode Island. Roger Williams had settled there after his banishment, so it was a logical destination for the displaced family. The Hutchinson family built a new life for themselves in Rhode Island, where they were free to worship as they chose.

Puritanical Clothing

Clothing varied a great deal in the seventeenth century according to a person's social class and occupation. Laborers and farmers usually wore leather vests and breeches, while merchants and judges might wear a waistcoat and shirt with a large linen collar.

Ships sailed regularly between the colonies and England, so eventually the clothing and fashions popular in the old country appeared in the stores in Boston. One mother in Ipswich wrote to her son in London to send her one of the latest neck fashions, a "lawn whiske." He wrote back to advise her that the "lawn whiske" was no longer in fashion, but he would send her a "black wifle" instead. Being a good son, he also sent her a feather fan, although he confessed that it might be out of style.

This kind of frivolous dress was frowned on by the Puritan ministers and other leaders in the Massachusetts Bay Colony. They issued rules of dress to curb what they saw as excess. Silver, gold, and silk laces were banned, as were beaver hats. In time short sleeves were banned as well to keep bare arms from showing.

In 1676, thirty-eight women were ordered to appear before the court for dressing in a wicked fashion. Sixteen-year-old Hannah Lyman was prosecuted for "wearing silk in a flaunting manner, in an offensive way and garb, not only before but when she stood presented, not only in Ordinary but Extraordinary times."[1] We can probably decipher from this statement that young Hannah dressed for court in a less-than-plain fashion.

Men had their finery as well. Red and green stockings were popular in New England, as were Monmouth or military cocked hats. Men sometimes carried muffs and certainly wore wigs in colonial days. The wigs they wore didn't look much like modern wigs, as they were powdered white. Most Puritans didn't approve of wigs for men any more than bare arms for women.

A woman wears a dress with a whisk around her neck (left) and a man wears a beaver hat and silk lace.

19

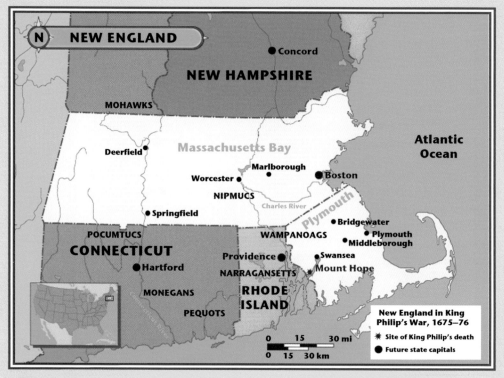

NEW ENGLAND

N

Concord

NEW HAMPSHIRE

MOHAWKS

Massachusetts Bay

Deerfield

Atlantic Ocean

Marlborough

Worcester

Boston

NIPMUCS

Charles River

Springfield

Plymouth

POCUMTUCS

WAMPANOAGS

Bridgewater

Plymouth

Middleborough

CONNECTICUT

Providence

Swansea

Hartford

Mount Hope

NARRAGANSETTS

MONEGANS

RHODE ISLAND

PEQUOTS

New England in King Philip's War, 1675–76

✳ Site of King Philip's death

● Future state capitals

0   15   30 mi

0   15   30 km

The Wampanoag Indians had been pushed westward by the expanding Plymouth Colony. During King Philip's War, the Wampanoags convinced the Nipmucs of central Massachusetts to become their allies. King Philip also got the Narragansetts of Rhode Island, who had been mortal enemies to the Wampanoags, to join him against the settlers.

Chapter

3

Changing Times in the Bay Colony

The flow of immigrants to Massachusetts slowed dramatically in 1640. King Charles I was forced to recall Parliament after eleven years of ruling without that body's interference. Civil war was threatening Britain, and Charles needed funds for defense. With Parliament back in session, some of the pressure on Puritans eased. Parliament forced Charles to repeal some of the laws he had enacted that had made immigration to America so attractive to Puritans.

This turn of events led to an economic slump in New England. Much of the economy of the Massachusetts Bay Colony was based on the steady influx of new residents who needed land and supplies when they arrived. With fewer newcomers, prices of everything dropped as demand decreased. A drop in prices is beneficial to consumers, but almost all the colonists supplied goods and services as well. They lost a lot of income.

The Massachusetts Bay General Court responded by setting prices on goods at what was considered a fair and just rate. They also fixed rents and wages. This manipulation was common in England but not so well liked in America. Winthrop and other Puritan leaders believed that the survival of the community was more important than any individual success. They saw this kind of working together as God's plan for mankind.

To Winthrop's dismay, many of his fellow colonists were more concerned with their own economic success than with any connection or obligation to the community. Winthrop wrote of his feelings in his journal during that time: "Indeed it was a very sad thing to see how little of a public spirit appeared in the country, but self-love too much."[1]

In spite of this lack of "public spirit," as Winthrop saw it, the economy gradually improved. Trade with other colonies and other countries became more important as ships flowed steadily in and out of Boston Harbor. By the 1650s, prosperity had returned to the Massachusetts Bay Colony.

However, there were other problems in the middle of the seventeenth century that hit at the heart of the Bay Colony. Religious diversity increased, and with it religious division became more common. Massachusetts Bay Colony had been founded as a Puritan colony where church and state were not separate. The first twenty years of its existence had seen compromises in this separation, but still it had retained its religiously guided government.

Many of the younger colonists who had been born in America stopped joining the church. Puritan rules and regulations didn't appeal to the younger generation. Neither had they known any religious persecution, however slight.

By the 1660s, church leaders saw declining membership as a real threat to their churches and communities. A conference or synod of Puritan ministers met in 1662 to figure out some solution to this problem. They proposed what became known as the Half-Way Covenant.

Membership in the Puritan church required a rather arduous process of self-examination and conversion. The Half-Way Covenant would sidestep the conversion issue and allow the children of members to become church members without requiring conversion. It was hoped that they would later become full members by way of conversion. The younger associate members would be part of the church, where they could be influenced for the better and could financially support the group. This financial support was a rather important aspect of the new covenant.

Each individual church had to vote on whether or not they wanted to allow the Half-Way Covenant. Some voted yes, and others were vehemently opposed to what they saw as a weakening of their faith. Nonetheless, this recruiting device was gradually adopted over the next forty years.

One of the most serious external threats to the well-being of the Massachusetts Bay Colony came in June 1675 with King Philip's War. King Philip's real name was Metacom. He was the son of Massasoit, chief of the Wampanoag Indians. Massasoit was the chief who had visited the Pilgrims and helped them. Metacom had been nicknamed King Philip because of his haughty ways.

Indians and settlers had coexisted rather peacefully considering the extreme differences in their chosen ways of life. There were often disagreements over land and animals, but most were settled without bloodshed.

When King Philip became chief, he was much less agreeable to the settlers than his father had been. Perhaps he saw that the advancement of the Europeans into Indian lands would never end. Hostilities started with an Indian attack on Swansea in Plymouth Colony, south of Boston. The Indians were likely upset about the execution of three braves who were found guilty of the murder of an Indian who had been friendly to the settlers. They may have also decided that the time was right to drive the settlers from their lands.

Messengers were sent to Boston, and soon a band of colonists marched out toward Indian country. Other men came from neighboring towns, and soon the forest rang with gunshots. Diplomatic measures were used, too, as messages were sent to the Narragansett Indians in Rhode Island and to the Pocumtucs in the Connecticut River Valley asking that they cooperate with the colonists. These Indian tribes had been friendly to the colonists in the past.

By the end of the summer, the situation had gotten worse. King Philip had persuaded both the Narragansetts and the Pocumtucs to join him. Philip's operation had become a drive to stop English settlement and show that the Indians were supreme in their native lands. By fall, the Nipmucs in the central uplands of Massachusetts Bay Colony joined

Metacom, known as King Philip, became chief of the Wampanoag Confederacy in 1662. A witness to the settlers' injustices toward his people, King Philip began a war against the settlers in 1675. After he was killed in 1676, his head was displayed on a pole at Plymouth—for 25 years.

the other Indians. Several western towns were burned, and the settlers who survived took refuge in Boston and other eastern towns.

The Indians had clearly won the first part of King Philip's War as the frontier settlements were abandoned. Yet the tide turned in winter as Governor Josiah Winslow of Plymouth Colony led militiamen from both colonies in an attack on the Narragansett camp in a swamp west of Narragansett Bay. A great battle took place, leaving between 700 and 800 Indians dead or wounded. The Narragansetts were broken, but the war didn't end.

Indian raids on settlements grew throughout the winter of 1676 as the Indians grew desperate for food. Many towns were attacked, leaving dozens of settlers dead or captured. By spring the Indians were on the defensive, and in August King Philip was shot dead at his home camp.

King Philip's War was over but the bloody results would impact the colony for years. The loss of life was staggering among both colonists and Indians, and destroyed property would take years to rebuild.

But the colonists had worked together against a common threat. As terrible as King Philip's War had been, it had been a test that the young colonies of Plymouth and Massachusetts Bay had passed. This ability to cooperate for a greater goal would serve them well later on.

Wampanoag Indians

When English colonists first came to America, the Wampanoag Indians lived in southeastern Massachusetts and eastern Rhode Island. The Wampanoags are known for befriending the Pilgrims, who founded Plymouth Colony in 1620. They helped the Pilgrims learn how to survive and celebrated the first harvest thanksgiving with them. According to Pilgrim William Bradford, the Indians brought five deer to the feast.

The Wampanoags lived in wigwams, which were small round houses built of small trees or saplings lashed together into a frame and covered with bark. Wampanoag women wove mats of bulrush, a plant that grew in the nearby marshes, and put them up around the inside of the house to help keep their homes warm in winter. The wigwams had holes in the very top for the smoke from the indoor fire to escape.

The villages were built around a central open space that the Wampanoags used for councils and ceremonies. Sometimes the villages were surrounded with a log wall for protection from their enemies. The men hunted deer, turkeys, and other small game; the women planted and harvested corn, squash, and beans. Children sometimes helped by gathering berries, nuts, and herbs.

The Wampanoags traveled on water in dugout canoes, which they made by hollowing out big trees. On land they simply walked from place to place. They were known for their beadwork and basket-making skills, and also for the wampum they made out of white and purple shells. Wampum was sometimes used for money and to commemorate special occasions. Designs and pictures on the wampum often told a story.

Wampum and shell

The Wampanoags' friendliness to the colonists didn't help them in the long run. The colonists often cheated the Indians and took their lands. The Europeans brought new and deadly diseases, including smallpox, which killed many of the Wampanoags. Today only the Aquinnah and Mishpee Wampanoag tribal groups maintain their presence on ancient tribal lands in Massachusetts.

Oliver Cromwell ruled England as Lord Protector after the English Civil Wars from 1653 until his death in 1658. In spite of Cromwell's inexperience as a soldier, he was very successful as a military man and essentially ruled England as a military dictator.

Chapter

England Reasserts Authority

In the 1650s, when Oliver Cromwell had been in power in England, British authority over its colonies decreased until it almost didn't exist. The Bay Colony had minted its own currency and was operating independently of the mother country. There was no particular desire to separate formally from England, because the ties were still strong and trading between the two continents flourished.

After the Stuarts were restored to power in 1660—when King Charles II was brought home from exile as the King of England—the English government had gradually sought to tighten controls over all of its colonies. The king and other English leaders wanted to benefit directly from the profits to be had in the colonies. They threatened to revoke the colony's charter.

In 1682, Bay Colony leaders sent Joseph Dudley to London to negotiate a new deal with the king that would allow them to keep the charter. Instead, Dudley secretly urged the king to get rid of the charter and give him a job in the new government. Thomas Hutchinson later said of Dudley that he possessed "as many virtues as can consist with so great a thirst for honor and power."[1] The charter was revoked in 1684.

Dudley wasn't the only Bay Colony leader who looked favorably on the new arrangement. Many businessmen thought they could profit handsomely by the new fees and other government favors that might come their way.

In 1685, Charles II died and his brother, the Duke of York, was crowned as James II. The new king founded the Dominion of New England to rule over its northern colonies in America. The Dominion would be based in Boston and administer Britain's interests in New Jersey, New York, Massachusetts, New Hampshire, Rhode Island, and Connecticut. This administration would control trade, land, and defense against the French, who had been challenging British claims in the New World.

The new setup showed its shortcomings within a year of its adoption. Sir Edmund Andros became governor of the Dominion of New England in December 1686. He got rid of the General Court, which had governed the Massachusetts Bay Colony from its beginning, and set new taxes. He outlawed town meetings except for the purpose of selecting town officials. Town meetings had been the heart of self-government in the Bay Colony, and forbidding them further crippled the colonists' ability to govern. He also threatened the landowners with quitrents, which were a type of tax that had never been collected in the Massachusetts Bay Colony because land grants had been awarded without further obligation.

In 1688, the Catholic James II was overthrown, and his Protestant daughter, Mary, and her husband, William of Orange, were made rulers of Great Britain. When this news arrived in Boston in April 1689, Boston citizens staged a coup and captured the detested Andros. Colony leaders took over the government, and the colony ran without a charter while a new one was negotiated with England.

Increase Mather, a Boston native, did much of the negotiating with King William, Queen Mary, and other British leaders. At last, in 1691, the new charter was approved; it took effect in 1692. It included two legislative houses and a legal system. Much of the government remained the same—the General Court would be reinstated—but there would be more political control by England. The new charter

William of Orange was a Dutch prince who married Mary, the daughter of King James II. A rebellion against King James brought William and Mary to the throne of England. They reigned jointly from 1689 to 1694, when Mary died. William was then the sole sovereign until his death in 1702.

also required more tolerance of other religious groups, such as Baptists, Anglicans, and Catholics.

One of the biggest changes brought about by the charter was that Plymouth Colony became part of the Massachusetts Bay Colony. Plymouth had existed independently since its founding but hadn't grown the way the neighboring colony of Massachusetts Bay had. Plymouth also hadn't sent enough representation or money to England to try to gain a new charter favorable to them.

What is now modern Maine was also affected by the new charter. Maine had been rather loosely part of Massachusetts since the 1630s, but the new charter made that association clear. Maine was part of Massachusetts until it was admitted to the union as a state in 1820.

The new royal governor, Sir William Phips (also spelled *Phipps*), arrived in Boston in May 1692 to find a full-blown crisis. He was greeted with the news that there was satanic business going on in Salem. Six girls, including the young daughter of the local minister, the Reverend

Samuel Parris, had accused several women of witchcraft. The girls said that the women had bewitched them.

Apparently the girls had been listening to stories told by Rev. Parris' slave Tituba, who had originally come from Barbados. At some point the harmless stories of fortunetelling and magic had taken on a deadly seriousness. The girls began having fits: they appeared to be out of their minds and acted in strange ways. They spoke nonsensical words and seemed to lose touch with the real world. A doctor examined them and, since they seemed physically normal, pronounced that they had been bewitched.

This pronouncement started a long road of accusations of witchcraft that led to the imprisonment of hundreds of people. The girls proclaimed that these people, almost all of them women, were attacking them and causing their fits.

Governor Phips was sympathetic to the Puritans in general, so he quickly appointed a special court to deal with the suspects. He then took himself off to Maine to oversee the army he had raised to fight the French.

The accusations eventually reached beyond Salem and into the surrounding towns. It seemed like an epidemic of witchcraft had gripped the countryside. Panic was just under the surface as even church members in good standing were accused. Sometimes the girls would insist that the prisoners be chained while in jail because that would keep them from further attack. Nineteen people were executed for the "crime."

One of the saddest stories was that of a four-year-old girl, Dorcas Good, who was imprisoned for nine months before being released. Her mother, Sarah, had been in the first group to be arrested in Salem and was executed in July 1692. The Salem girls said that a specter of this little girl had attacked them, inflicting bites on their arms. When Dorcas was set before the afflicted girls, they went into spasms of what appeared to be intense pain. Dorcas was ordered put in irons and sent to jail. Special irons had to be made to fit her small wrists and ankles. She was released in December 1692, but, according to her father, she was never the same after her ordeal.

The jails were full and many others awaited charges at home before the communities came to their senses. Finally here and there

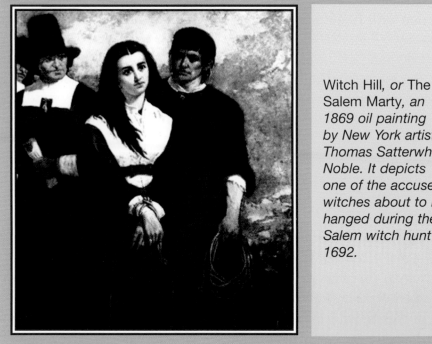

Witch Hill, *or* The Salem Marty, *an 1869 oil painting by New York artist Thomas Satterwhite Noble. It depicts one of the accused witches about to be hanged during the Salem witch hunt of 1692.*

men began to speak out against the trials. The last execution was held in September 1692.

The General Court came tardily to the conclusion that something was amiss when so many people stood accused of witchcraft. In January a trial was held for fifty-six of the prisoners. All but three were found not guilty.

In May, Governor Phips issued a release for any accused or condemned persons remaining in jail. Under the law, prisoners still had to pay fees upon their release. Some of the accused lingered in jail until they could arrange payment.

What would become one of the most serious stains on the reputation of the Massachusetts Bay Colony had come to a boiling point and then subsided. What happened to the young women accusers remains a mystery, even after hundreds of years of study and speculation.

In less than a decade, much had happened to the Massachusetts Bay Colony: the Andros governorship, the new charter, and the Salem witch hunt. During the remainder of the seventeenth century and into the early years of the eighteenth, the colony moved toward a stronger connection with England—and that move would bring prosperity to the Bay Colony.

The religious tolerance dictated by the charter of 1692 had diluted the Puritan influence. Boston prided itself on its broad-minded acceptance of different religions and their beliefs. Many wanted to leave their pious Puritan heritage behind, although there were those who spoke longingly of the early days of the colony when life was simpler. Even in the countryside, the old ways gradually changed, with the original Puritan emphasis weakening. This trend reversed in the 1730s as a religious revival called the Great Awakening swept through New England.

The revival started in Northampton, Massachusetts, with the preaching of Reverend Jonathan Edwards in 1734. He spoke of submitting to the will of God and called on people to rely on God's power—rather than on good deeds or behavior—for redemption. Edwards' words, with his fiery delivery, spoke to the hearts of his community. Hundreds of new people joined the church.

Edwards wrote of this Northampton revival, and the phenomenon spread throughout the colony. In 1740, English evangelist George Whitefield arrived in Boston. His preaching converted hundreds there, and he went on to tour Massachusetts and Connecticut. Whitefield's preaching style was quite different from what Puritans were accustomed to. He used emotional appeals to stir the people to action.

The emphasis on emotion in religious practice also stirred much dissent. This new religious fervor set much store by individual judgment rather than the expert reason of ordained clergymen or preachers. The Puritan ministers did not abide by such preaching. Many churches became divided when congregations couldn't agree. They would split apart to become two or more separate groups.

The Massachusetts Bay Colony in 1740 was vastly different from what it had been 100 years before. It was a prosperous land with abundant natural resources. The colonists wanted to find further wealth through trade with England and the rest of its empire. The colony wasn't looking for independence from England yet, but the next twenty years would change its outlook.

Increase Mather

Increase Mather was a Puritan clergyman whose father, Richard Mather, and son, Cotton Mather, were also ministers. Between the three Mathers, Massachusetts received almost a century of leadership. Increase graduated from Harvard University in 1656 and soon moved to Ireland, where he studied at Trinity College. He became a chaplain to an English garrison and served there until he returned to Massachusetts in 1661.

He began preaching at Old North Church of Boston and was eventually ordained there. Mather held that position for the rest of his life. He became president of Harvard College, although he was not often in residence there.

Mather was chosen by the Massachusetts General Court to go to England in 1688 to represent the colony's interests. The king and Parliament had demanded that the Bay Colony give up their charter, and Mather went to negotiate. He was instrumental in obtaining a new charter for Massachusetts that preserved many of their rights. Mather didn't keep Plymouth Colony from becoming a part of Massachusetts Bay Colony, but he did keep it from being annexed by New York.

Salem witch trials

Increase Mather played an important role in the Salem witch trials, as he was one of the first ministers to speak out against the trials. His son Cotton was also involved in the trials, and both men eventually developed doubts that the trials were fair. Father and son believed in the existence of witchcraft, and both wrote widely about their beliefs. They just didn't think the evidence presented in Salem was credible.

Increase visited many of the accused witches in prison, and several of them took back their confessions, saying that they had been forced to plead guilty. Toward the end of the trials he published *Cases of Conscience Concerning Evil Spirits*. In this writing he questioned whether the young girls who claimed to have been possessed were telling the truth. He also questioned the confessions and the evidence presented.

The aftermath of the Salem trials undermined Mather's authority somewhat, but he remained a powerful figure in colonial history until his death in 1723.

The first battle of the French and Indian War was fought in Nova Scotia in what was then French Canada. Later battles took place at Niagara and Lake Champlain. The final victories that drove the French out of Canada took place at Quebec and at Montreal in 1760.

Chapter

5

A New Nation

Ties to Britain were strong during the middle of the eighteenth century in the Massachusetts Bay Colony. This was particularly apparent during the French and Indian War, which began in America in 1754. The French and their Indian allies had attempted to press into the interior of Pennsylvania and found a settlement there, on the site of present-day Pittsburgh.

Massachusetts contributed thousands of militiamen to fight the French and Indian War. Some were independent units, and some were attached to the British regulars. The first military action by the colonists took place in spring 1755. The royal governor, William Shirley, sent 2,000 Massachusetts militiamen eastward to repel the French in Nova Scotia. At the same time, Shirley sent another 2,000 troops westward to attack French forts at Crown Point on Lake Champlain and at Niagara. The militia was successful in driving back the French in Nova Scotia, but the western campaign didn't succeed.

A few hundred Massachusetts men were attached to the British regulars in the battles that finally led to victory over the French. The British won at Quebec in April 1760, and the final victory came at Montreal in September. France was forced to cede all of Canada to the British.

Massachusetts soldiers had become known for their willingness to defend their colony. Governor Thomas Pownall gave high praise to the troops when he reported to authorities in England. He wrote that Massachusetts was "the frontier and advanced guard of all the colonies against the enemy in Canada."[1]

With the Treaty of Paris in 1763, signed by Britain, France, Spain, and Portugal, over seventy years of fighting for dominance in North America was ended. Massachusetts Bay Colony was proud of its mother country and how Britain had banished the French.

Once the long years of war with France were over, Great Britain decided to reorganize its administration of the American colonies. Britain had spent millions of dollars defending their lands in America. The British king and Parliament thought it only seemed right that the colonies should help pay the debts left over from the wars.

In 1764, Parliament passed a new version of an old tax on molasses. Molasses was used to make rum and was important to the economy of several of the New England colonies. Up until this point, collection had been spotty, and most merchants were able to avoid paying the tax. The tax on molasses was decreased, but now Britain intended to strictly enforce its collection.

This new law, called the Sugar Act, disrupted trade with other foreign markets. But this tax was only the first strike from the mother country. In March 1765, Parliament passed yet another act designed solely to raise money rather than regulate trade.

The Stamp Act required that the colonists buy special stamps to put on legal, business, and other documents. The actual economic impact would probably have been small, but the intent struck at the heart of the liberties that Massachusetts Bay colonists had long held dear.

A young lawyer named John Adams drafted his town's sentiments into a document of instructions to their representative in the legislature. The Braintree Instructions, named for the town, became a model for similar documents written on behalf of other communities. The first sentence of the Instructions contained the simplest explanation for the uproar created in the colonies by the Stamp Act. "We have always understood it to be a grand and fundamental principle of the constitution, that no freeman should be subject to any tax to which he has not given his own consent, in person or by proxy."[2]

Since it was impractical for the American colonies to be represented in Parliament, it was reasonable that they should assess their own taxes as they saw fit. Bay Colony leaders and others throughout the British colonies felt that this right of no taxation without representation was guaranteed to them by that great English document of law, the Magna Carta.

After months of protests, the Stamp Act was repealed, and hope rose in the colonies that this would be the end of the taxation issue. Hope died quickly as a series of other taxes and restrictions were imposed over the next few years. King George III and Parliament were determined to gain better control over and collect taxes from their troublesome colonies in America.

Protests gradually increased, with occasional outbursts of violence directed against representatives of the British government. Boston was a hotbed for the building resentment against Britain. Two of the most outspoken radicals, Samuel Adams and John Hancock, lived in Boston. They helped form the Sons of Liberty, which was a secret organization devoted to securing independence for the colonies.

In the summer of 1768, Boston reached a boiling point as townspeople objected to the collection of the latest taxes imposed by the Townshend Acts. There were several small riots and many disagreements between the colonists and the officials collecting the fees. In September 1768, British troops were sent to Boston to keep order.

The Boston residents did everything they could to make the British soldiers' lives miserable. Insults were exchanged, and sometimes fistfights broke out. After about a year and a half, tensions boiled over on March 5, 1770.

That evening, townspeople and soldiers had been yelling at each other and sometimes fighting. A small mob of townspeople started throwing rocks and ice at a British soldier standing guard. The mob, which had grown to fifty or sixty people, refused to leave the area when reinforcements arrived. Eight soldiers faced the mob as the crowd insulted the soldiers and hit them with sticks.

When one soldier was knocked down, he fired his musket. The other soldiers fired too. Five colonists were killed and several others were wounded. Samuel Adams, in his continuing quest to stir up rebellion, labeled this event the Boston Massacre.

The next couple of years were relatively quiet in the colonies. Parliament repealed most of the taxes in the Townshend Acts except for the tax on tea. This tax continued to rile the Boston merchants, and on December 16, 1773, the Sons of Liberty did something about it.

The Boston Tea Party was a well-planned demonstration against the tea tax. The Sons of Liberty, poorly disguised as Indians, boarded a British ship anchored in Boston Harbor. They tossed crates of tea overboard to protest the tax. The Boston Tea Party was successful in rousing popular opinion against the British, who soon took action.

General Thomas Gage had been appointed governor of Massachusetts. He arrived in the spring to close Boston Harbor until the Bostonians paid for the ruined tea. The Harbor was closed to all but British Navy ships. The city still refused to pay. Meanwhile, food and other necessities were smuggled overland into Boston from nearby ports.

Parliament passed more laws restricting freedom in Massachusetts. Called the Intolerable Acts, these laws allowed only the governor to appoint judges. Jury members were to be appointed by the sheriff. The General Court or legislative representatives were to be chosen by the king.

At last the other colonies agreed that they should meet to talk over their common problems with Britain. The First Continental Congress met in Philadelphia in September 1774. Paul Revere rode back and forth from Boston to Philadelphia several times to communicate with the Congress. The radical leaders in Boston sent word that they had advised towns in Massachusetts Bay Colony to organize their own governments and militias.

The Continental Congress decided to boycott British products and supported Massachusetts' call for towns to form militias. Most delegates weren't yet ready to declare independence, but they saw that preparation was necessary. They adjourned to implement their plans and scheduled another meeting for the spring of 1775.

Samuel Adams (left) and John Hancock were important figures in the American Revolution and the forming of the United States of America. They helped organize and carry out the Boston Tea Party with other Sons of Liberty. Hancock was the first person to sign the Declaration of Independence, and he signed it largely and clearly. Both men served as governor of Massachusetts after the war.

Before the Second Continental Congress could convene in May, revolution came to Massachusetts. Governor Gage had been ordered to arrest opposition leaders, including Samuel Adams and John Hancock, and to seize gunpowder.

On April 18, 1775, Gage ordered about 700 of his best soldiers to get ready to move out in search of Adams, Hancock, and the gunpowder. They set out late that night in boats to cross the Charles River. This was the occasion for Paul Revere's famous ride to alert the countryside that the British were coming.

The local elite militias, who sometimes called themselves minutemen because they could respond so quickly, gathered first at Lexington on the village green. When the British arrived, the two groups marched at each other, waiting for their opponents to fire first. Finally someone did fire, but it was never known which side fired first. Shooting continued until eight of the militiamen were killed and several others were wounded.

The British marched on to Concord, where they seized the gunpowder and military equipment. They weren't able to get rid of the militia so easily. Hundreds of Patriots had poured into Concord to defend the village. They fired at the British and chased them all the way back to Boston, picking off redcoats on their way.

Fifty militiamen died that day or later from wounds; ninety British soldiers died or were reported missing. It was a decisive stroke by the Americans and must have given Governor Gage something to think about.

June brought still more trouble when Gage ordered his troops to attack what appeared to be American fortifications on nearby Breeds and Bunker Hills. On June 17, the troops attacked the Americans in a bloody battle as the militiamen shot from trenches dug in the ground. Eventually the British troops drove back the Americans, but the British lost many more soldiers than the Americans had.

Boston was liberated in March 1776 by the newly formed Continental Army headed by George Washington. Washington surrounded the city with cannon and waited. British General Howe prepared to attack the American positions but apparently changed his mind and withdrew to the city of Halifax in Nova Scotia.

Boston was free of its tormentors, and the British never attempted to return. Massachusetts Bay colonists were finally free to build a state. They needed no convincing that independence was the right thing for America. Most residents had believed that for many years and had worked to bring the other colonies around to their viewpoint.

By the summer of 1776, while the Declaration of Independence was being written and approved in Philadelphia, Massachusetts had started to rebuild its local governments and courts.

Once the British left Boston, there was no more significant fighting in the colony. Massachusetts participated in all the decision making of the colonies and provided what help it could for the Continental Army,

Paintings of famous historical events are often more dramatic than accurate. Hy Hintermeister's painting of Paul Revere setting off on his famous ride is one example of dramatic presentation. Revere had quietly rowed across the river in the darkness to avoid the notice of the British. It's doubtful that he allowed any fanfare when he left, and he may not have talked to anyone but the people who supplied his horse on the Charlestown side.

but it escaped further destruction by the British Army. Massachusetts Patriots had played their part well.

The preamble to Massachusetts' new constitution, which was ratified in 1780, set out what government must provide for its people. People were to be able to enjoy "in safety and tranquility their natural rights and the blessings of life."[3]

This promise was not so different than the hopes that John Winthrop had had for his colony in 1630.

Paul Revere's Midnight Ride

Paul Revere was a silver-smith in Boston in 1775 when war with Britain seemed inevitable. As a member of the Sons of Liberty, Revere had served as a messenger for the radicals in Boston. While he ran his business, he kept an eye on the British soldiers stationed in Boston.

In April 1775, it looked as if the British were planning something. He suspected that the redcoats would soon be dispatched to seize the colonists' arms and gunpowder. Revere traveled to Concord to warn the residents to hide their arms and valuables. Back in Boston, he met with Patriot leaders to finalize their own plans should the British make a move.

It was agreed that Revere would place signal lanterns in the tower of Old North Church in Boston. The lights could be seen across the Charles River in Charlestown. One light would signify that the British were moving out by land across the Boston Neck and northwest to Concord. Two lights would mean that the British were crossing the Charles River in boats and going west to Concord.

Revere waited. On the evening of April 18, word came that the British were preparing boats to cross the Charles. Revere's associates hung two lanterns in the tower, while Revere quietly rowed to Charleston to a waiting horse. Meanwhile another messenger, William Dawes, had been sent the long way around to Concord through Roxbury and Brookline.

Revere rode out of Charlestown on a perilous trip through the countryside to Lexington, where he met Dawes and a third man, Dr. Samuel Prescott. They warned Samuel Adams and John Hancock, who were staying in Lexington, and rode on toward Concord. Both Dawes and Revere were captured, but Prescott delivered the message to Concord.

When he was questioned by the British officers, Revere gave them false information about the number of militiamen waiting at Concord. They released him so that they could warn their fellow troops. On his return to Lexington, Revere heard shots and knew that the Revolutionary War had begun.

Chapter Notes

Chapter 1
"The Citty Upon a Hill"

1. Darrett Rutman, *Winthrop's Boston* (Chapel Hill: The University of North Carolina Press, 1965), p. 23.
2. Ibid.
3. Ibid. p. 4.
4. John Winthrop, *The History of New England* (New York: Arno Press, 1972), pp. 44–45.

Chapter 3
Changing Times in the Bay Colony

1. Darrett Rutman, *Winthrop's Boston* (Chapel Hill: The University of North Carolina Press, 1965), p. 245.

Chapter 4
England Reasserts Authority

1. Richard Brown, *Massachusetts* (New York: W.W. Norton & Company, Inc., 1978), p. 54.

Chapter 5
A New Nation

1. Benjamin Labaree, *Colonial Massachusetts* (Millwood, New York: KTO Press, 1979), p. 212.
2. James Peabody, editor, *John Adams, a Biography in His Own Words* (New York: Newsweek Press, 1973), p. 93.
3. Labaree, p. 309.

Chronology

1620	Pilgrims arrive in Massachusetts Bay and found Plymouth Colony.
1630	John Winthrop arrives in Salem to found Massachusetts Bay Colony.
1636	Roger Williams is banished by the Puritans and founds Providence (Rhode Island).
1637	Anne Hutchinson is convicted of heresy and banished.
1640	The Great Migration slows to a trickle.
1657	Governor William Bradford dies.
1662	The Half-Way Covenant is proposed to help increase church membership.
1675	King Philip's War is fought in Plymouth and Massachusetts Bay Colonies.
1685	James II founds the Dominion of New England.
1689	A new charter for the colony is negotiated. It takes effect in 1692.
1692	The Salem witch trials begin.
1740	The Great Awakening begins.
1754	The French and Indian War, between France and England, begins in North America.
1763	The Treaty of Paris ends the war between France and England.
1764	Parliament passes the Sugar Act.
1765	The Stamp Act is passed.
1768	Boston is occupied by British troops.
1770	Five civilians are killed by British soldiers in what the Patriots will call the Boston Massacre.
1773	Patriots dump a shipment of tea into the harbor at the Boston Tea Party.
1775	The Battles of Lexington and Concord are fought. The Battle of Bunker Hill is fought at Breed's Hill.
1776	Boston is liberated by the Continental Army.
1780	The state of Massachusetts ratifies its new constitution.
1820	The state of Maine is admitted to the Union as part of the Missouri Compromise.

Timeline in History

1577	Francis Drake sets out with five ships to sail around the world.
1580	John Dee, English mathematician, invents the crystal ball.
1585	The first English colony is founded at Roanoke, Virginia.
1590	The microscope is invented.
1607	Jamestown Colony is founded in Virginia.
1637	Cardinal Richelieu of France creates the first table knife.
1646	Roger Scott is tried in Massachusetts for sleeping in church.
1649	Charles I is beheaded for treason.
1665	At least 68,000 Londoners die of the bubonic plague.
1670	A cafe in Paris begins serving ice cream.
1700	After a strong earthquake in California, a deadly tsunami hits Japan.
1742	The first indoor swimming pool opens in London.
1751	The first American hospital is founded in Pennsylvania.
1769	Daniel Boone explores the land that will become Tennessee.
1777	Vermont declares itself an independent republic and becomes the first American colony to abolish slavery.
1792	Gas lighting is developed in Scotland.
1795	Beethoven makes his debut in Vienna as a pianist.
1800	The White House is completed.
1805	The Lewis and Clark Expedition reaches the Pacific Ocean.
1811	The New Madrid Earthquakes strike along the Mississippi River.
1812	The U.S. fights Britain for sea rights in the War of 1813.
1861	The U.S. Civil War begins.

Further Reading

For Young Adults

Anderson, Dale. *The American Revolution*. Austin, Texas: Raintree Steck-Vaughn Publishers, 2003.

Clark, Beth. *Anne Hutchinson, Religious Leader*. Philadelphia: Chelsea House Publishers, 2000.

Dow, George Francis. *Everyday Life in the Massachusetts Bay Colony*. New York: Dover Publications, Inc., 1935, 1988.

Gibson, Karen Bush. *The Life and Times of Samuel Adams*. Hockessin, DE: Mitchell Lane Publishers, 2007.

Hinman, Bonnie. *Thomas Gage, British General*. Philadelphia: Chelsea House Publishers, 2002.

Kent, Deborah. *The American Revolution, "Give Me Liberty, or Give Me Death!"* Hillside, NJ: Enslow Publishers, Inc. 1994.

Randolph, Ryan. *Paul Revere and the Minutemen of the American Revolution*. New York: PowerPlus Books, 2002.

Works Consulted

Brown, Richard. *Massachusetts*. New York: W. W. Norton & Company, Inc., 1978.

Earle, Alice Morse. *Customs and Fashions in Old New England*. Rutland, VT: Charles E. Tuttle Company, 1893, 1973.

Forbes, Esther. *Paul Revere & the World He Lived In*. Boston: Houghton Mifflin Company, 1942.

Hall, David, editor. *Puritanism in Seventeenth-Century Massachusetts*. New York: Holt, Rinehart and Winston, 1968.

Labaree, Benjamin. *Colonial Massachusetts*. Millwood, New York: KTO Press, 1979.

Morison, Samuel Eliot. *Builders of the Bay Colony*. Boston: Houghton Mifflin Company, 1930.

Morgan, Edmund. *The Puritan Dilemma: The Story of John Winthrop*. Boston: Little, Brown and Company, 1958.

Peabody, James, editor. *John Adams, a Biography in His Own Words*. New York: Newsweek Book Division, 1973.

Robinson, Enders. *Salem Witchcraft and Hawthorne's House of the Seven Gables*. Bowie, MD: Heritage Books, Inc., 1992.

Rutman, Darrett. *Winthrop's Boston*. Chapel Hill: The University of North Carolina Press, 1965.

Schweninger, Lee. *John Winthrop*. Boston: Twayne Publishers, 1990.

Winthrop, John. *The History of New England from 1630 to 1649*. New York: Arno Press, 1972.

On the Internet

Pilgrim Hall Museum
http://www.pilgrimhall.org/ plgrmhll.htm

Anne Hutchinson
http://www.annehutchinson.com/

"Religious Freedom: The Trial of Anne Hutchinson"
http://pbskids.org/wayback/ civilrights/features_hutchison.html

Wampanoag Tribe of Gay Head (Aquinnah)
http://www.wampanoagtribe.net/Pages/ Wampanoag_ACC/index

Glossary

constables
(KON-stuh-buls)
Police officers in a small town or village.

diversity
(dih-VUR-seh-tee)
Different kinds or sorts.

fortnight
(FORT-nyt)
A period of two weeks.

heretic
(HAIR-eh-tik)
Someone who holds beliefs that don't agree with the church's beliefs.

heirarchy
(HY-er-ar-kee)
Church government by a group of officials who are organized by rank, such as the bishops in the Catholic Church.

nonsensical
(non-SEN-seh-kul)
Words or actions that have no meaning.

Orthodox
(OR-theh-doks)
Closely following an agreed-upon belief system.

peninsula
(peh-NIN-suh-luh)
A piece of land surrounded on nearly all sides by water.

persecuted
(PER-seh-kyoo-ted)
Continually treated in a cruel or harsh way because of race, religion, political ideas, or some other difference.

proxy
(PRAK-see)
Officially standing in for or representing someone who cannot be there in person.

recruiting
(ree-KROO-ting)
Convincing new members to join an organization.

repealed
(rih-PEELD)
Doing away with or canceling officially.

revocation
(reh-vuh-KAY-shun)
A cancellation or withdrawing.

specter
(SPEK-ter)
A ghost.

waistcoat
(WAYST-koht)
An ornamental vest worn under a tight-fitting jacket.

Index